YOUR KNOWLEDGE HAS VALUE

Bibliographic information published by the German National Library:

The German National Library lists this publication in the National Bibliography; detailed bibliographic data are available on the Internet at http://dnb.dnb.de .

Imprint:

Copyright © 2015 GRIN Verlag, Open Publishing GmbH
Print and binding: Books on Demand GmbH, Norderstedt Germany
ISBN: 9783668215573

This book at GRIN:

http://www.grin.com/en/e-book/322150/in-what-way-does-isomorphism-caused-by-western-donors-influence-effectiveness

Stefanie Brandl

Aus der Reihe: e-fellows.net stipendiaten-wissen

e-fellows.net (Hrsg.)

Band 1788

In what way does isomorphism caused by western donors influence effectiveness of non-governmental organizations in Africa?

GRIN Publishing

GRIN - Your knowledge has value

Since its foundation in 1998, GRIN has specialized in publishing academic texts by students, college teachers and other academics as e-book and printed book. The website www.grin.com is an ideal platform for presenting term papers, final papers, scientific essays, dissertations and specialist books.

Visit us on the internet:

http://www.grin.com/

http://www.facebook.com/grincom

http://www.twitter.com/grin_com

Management and Organization Theories through the Lens
of Mission-Driven Organizations
Summer Term 2015

Term Paper

Chair for Corporate Sustainability Management

In what way does isomorphism caused by western donors influence effectiveness of non-governmental organizations in Africa?

Deadline: 10.08.2015

Stefanie Brandl
Word Count: 4.034

Abstract

This paper examines in what way isomorphism caused by western donors influences the effectiveness of non-governmental organizations in Africa. As about 40 % of the population in Sub-Saharan Africa live below the poverty line it is interesting to know if African NGOs work effectively. For that institutional theory as well as the conceptualizations of effectiveness, goal attainment, resource acquisition and reputation, are applied to find out the influence of isomorphism on the management, program, environment and partnership domain of NGOs. It is concluded that without donors many NGOs could not exist. Nevertheless NGOs became local managers of foreign aid money, not managers of local African development processes and are too much influenced by donors.

Table of contents

List of abbreviations

ECNGOC	Eastern Cape NGO Coalition
NGO	Non-governmental organization
INGO	International non-governmental organization
OECD	Organization for Economic Co-operation and Development
UNICEF	United Nations International Children's Emergency Fund

Table of figures

1. Trend of homogenization

Usually organizations try to differentiate through own missions, however, they become more alike. That can be explained i.e. through political influences and the aim for legitimacy, imitation in case of uncertainty and people having similar educational backgrounds (DiMaggio & Powell, 1983). Di Maggio and Powell declare this homogenization as isomorphism. Particularly in projects, strategies and governance structures of non-governmental organizations (NGOs) isomorphism is prevalent, caused by the international aid system (Claeyé & Jackson, 2012; Kontinen, 2005). Does that paradox come up because isomorphism caused by Western donors leads to more effectiveness in the involved organizations? The question will be analyzed using the example of African NGOs receiving funds from Western donors. The paper concentrates on NGOs as up to now, research in organizational theory focused mainly on firms, governments and schools (Rauh, 2010). Yet, as about 40 % of the population in Sub-Saharan Africa live below the poverty line (United Nations, 2013) and since it is the donors' expectation, it is particularly important to analyze if African NGOs work effectively.

To answer the above mentioned question first the terms NGO and aid delivery system are clarified in chapter 2.1. Thereon, characteristics of African NGOs will be derived and the term effectiveness will be defined in chapter 2.2 and 2.3 before the institutional theory will be introduced in chapter 3. The focus will lay on the three types of isomorphism as well as on explaining an organizational field. Finally in chapter 4 the theoretical concept of institutional theory and the model to measure effectiveness will be applied to African NGOs.

2. Introducing the aid delivery system, African non-governmental organizations and the term effectiveness

2.1 Aid delivery system

To answer the question if isomorphism caused by Western donors leads to more effectiveness in non-governmental organizations first the terms NGO and aid delivery system are explained. NGOs are defined as "self-governing, private, not-for-profit organizations that are geared to improving the quality of life of disadvantaged people." (Vakil, 1997, p. 2060). Out of many, this definition was chosen as it best shows the NGOs' focus on their mission of serving people, which is - according to Burger and Owens - their main aim. NGOs focus i.e. on poverty alleviation, sustainable development, human rights, health, women empowerment, education or rural development.

For an overview of the aid delivery system the model of Burger and Owens, that presents the three-agent relationship between donors, NGOs and the local community, has been expanded by adding INGOs (international NGOs) and donor agencies, as money is often not transferred directly but via these organizations. Moreover, governments in the home country of NGOs as well as in the developing country play an important role as they regulate NGOs (Madon, 1999; Nelson, 2006). The aid delivery system is presented in Figure 1. (1) Donors mostly from high-income countries give money to (2) international non-governmental organizations, like Oxfam, Action Aid or Save the Children, which cooperate with (3) intermediate NGOs to provide help to (4) beneficiaries in low-income countries (Madon, 1999; Nelson, 2006). There are individuals donating and formal fund provider. The difference between both is that first mentioned donate directly to local programs while the latter usually request NGOs to monitor performance targets as a prerequisite for their donations (Smith, 2004). Formal fund provider are i.e. governmental or multilateral donor agencies, foundations, trade unions and faith-based organizations (Rauh, 2010). The best known are multilateral agencies like UNICEF, the

World Bank and the Organization for Economic Co-operation and Development (OECD) which spend money to the government of the developing country or INGOs which than get in contact with intermediate NGOs (Foli & Béland, 2014; World Bank, 1995). In this paper donors are defined as formal fund provider who request monitoring and reporting.

Figure 1: Aid delivery system

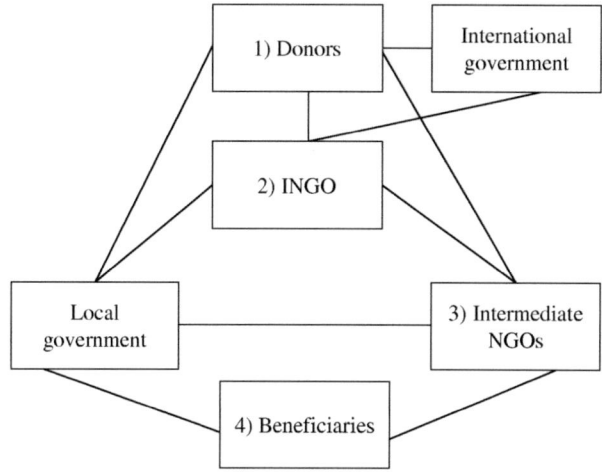

Source: modelled after Burger & Owens, 2013; Madon, 1999, p. 258

2.2 African non-governmental organizations

To evaluate the effectiveness of African NGOs, it is necessary to understand how they operate. Therefore their characteristics like the organizational structure and the dimensions, as well as the working conditions in Africa, are briefly explained.

According to Kontinen (2005) the structure of NGOs was often copied from i.e. religious organizations and commercial enterprises. It was designed for the registration of the NGO but not practical in use. Nevertheless, in most cases there was an executive committee, responsible for daily business, different departments like finance, administration and operations, as well as offices. The founder members, Kontinen states, often came from one family, ethnic network or professional network. NGOs are divided into six dimensions: value, technic, resource, human, politics and law. The values of NGOs are mirrored in their mission, which is achieved with the right skills and organizational assets, like expertise and capacities (technic), along with resources and the sourcing strategy itself (resource). Moreover, there are relationships within and among organizations (human) but also informal ties through networks or alliances (politics). The legal dimension demonstrates statutory, regulatory, contractual and other formal arrangements (law) (Nelson, 2006). Furthermore, it is important to look at the environment the African NGOs works in. Africa is characterized by a low level of economic development, unpredictable factors and a high level of corruption. Often African employees do not follow instructions, deliver poor quality, do not innovate because it is not expected, respond to problems only when they come up and often come late because relationships are more important than timeliness and efficiency (Muturi & Parris, 2013). According to Michael (2004) NGOs reflect usual weaknesses of African civil society.

2.3 Three conceptualizations of effectiveness

After introducing the aid delivery system and the characteristics of African NGOs the term effectiveness has to be clarified. In general efficiency stands for doing the things right, choosing proper means and focusing on the present whereas effectiveness stands for doing the right things, heading for an end and focusing on long-term. Nevertheless both are needed to be successful as efficiency drives effectiveness and is mostly not the end objective (Sudit, 1996). The paper focuses on effectiveness setting the output in relation to NGOs´ end objectives. Since little data is available for the input factor which would be required to calculate efficiency and as effectiveness is more important to explain the African working conditions (cf. 2.2) efficiency is not taken into consideration.

Effectiveness will be measured according to a framework of Lecy, Swedlund and Schmitz (2012). The researchers concluded that there is no consensus on a definition for NGOs´ effectiveness. That is why they came up with a new model combining four dominant domains of research: (1) Organizational management means improving the NGOs´ own management effectiveness. (2) Program design and implementation represent the impact of programs including the improvement of aid delivery and their ability to help. (3) Global and political norms and the donor system represent the NGOs´ environment. Here the NGOs capability to secure resources, build networks and protect against threats is inspected. Moreover, the audit culture, transparency and legitimation as well as the external influences that affect NGOs are looked at. (4) Concerning networks and partnerships between i.e. governments, Western donors and NGOs, NGOs are challenged to mobilize others and work effectively with people of different cultures, values and expectations. Lecy et al related these four to earlier "effectiveness approaches" namely goal attainment, resource acquisition and reputation and so created a combined effectiveness measurement model. Figure 2 demonstrates that management is effective if goals are met, if recourses are brought up and if a good reputation is gained. For the environment´s effectiveness the resource and the reputational approach are best. Advantages of this model are the user-friendliness and a better capturing of relational aspects of effectiveness (Lecy, Schmitz, & Swedlund, 2012).

Figure 2: Combined effectiveness measurement model

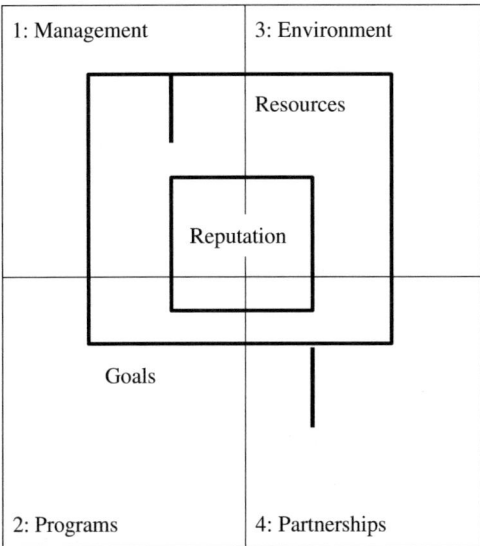

1: Management	3: Environment
	Resources
Reputation	
Goals	
2: Programs	4: Partnerships

Source: Lecy et al., 2012, p. 36

3. Institutional theory

3.1 Types of isomorphism

After introducing the aid delivery system, African NGOs and the tool used to measure their effectiveness, institutional theory – applied to answer the research question – will be explained.

"Institutional theory attempts to provide a conceptual lens for organizational action." (Sellers, Fogarty, & Parker, 2012, p. 182). Actors try to change their organizations (North, 1990) but in the end they become more alike. This homogenization can be explained by institutional isomorphism which is conferring to Hawley (1968) a "constraining process that forces one unit in a population to resemble other units that face the same set of environmental conditions" (DiMaggio & Powell, 1983, p. 149). A distinction can be made between institutional and competitive isomorphism (Fennell, 1980; Meyer & Hannan, 1979). The focus of this paper lays on institutional isomorphism as it focuses on legitimacy (Carroll & Delacroix, 1982) which is for NGOs more important than competition as it enables getting support and grants (Hager, Galaskiewicz, Bielefeld, & Pins, 1996). There are three mechanisms describing institutional isomorphic change: 1) Coercive isomorphism resulting from political influence and aiming for legitimacy. Pressures by other organizations, upon which the company is dependent, expectations from society, environmental regulations or reporting requirements lead to homogenization. 2) Mimetic isomorphism, the modeling and imitating of other organizations, is an answer to uncertainty. Especially employees, consulting firms and industry trade associations can diffuse models. 3) Normative isomorphism is caused by professionalization which means norms developed during education. This can be either in universities or in professional networks. Moreover, the hiring process and typical career paths such as assistant, associate and professor lead to normative isomorphism as in the fight for talented employees an organization feels pressure to provide the programs and services offered by other organizations (DiMaggio & Powell, 1983).

3.2 Organizational field

To analyze the effectiveness of isomorphism, the NGOs' organizational field - including players, intermediators and beneficiaries - is identified. According to DiMaggio and Powell an organizational field is formed by organizations "that, in the aggregate, constitute a recognized area of institutional life: key suppliers, resource and product consumers, regulatory agencies [...] [and competitors]" (DiMaggio & Powell, 1983, 1983, p. 148). In this field, institutions are the rules of the game while organizations are the players. Institutions can be created or come up over time and differ depending on the country (North, 1990). According to DiMaggio and Powell, a field only exists if it is institutionally defined, that means if it fulfills the following four aspects, namely the rise of interaction among organizations in the field, the existence of inter-organizational structures, the rise of information and the awareness to be part of a common enterprise.

To identify the players of the field the stakeholder approach of Freeman is used. Freeman (2010, p. 46) described stakeholder as "any group or individual who can affect or is affected by the achievement of the organization's objectives" and differentiates between primary and secondary stakeholders. Primary stakeholders, the most important stakeholder of NGOs, are donors, employees, the management and the advisory board, and beneficiaries, which are kind of customers of the NGO. Secondary stakeholders are governments, media, influential local elites, outside consultants and public administrators. To demonstrate the dependencies Figure 1 was expanded (Figure 3). Without donors many projects could not be realized so that they are the most important stakeholder group. In this paper the most important stakeholders are employees, the advisory board and beneficiaries as they benefit most from donations.

Figure 3: Organizational field of NGOs

Blue = primary stakeholder, white = secondary stakeholder

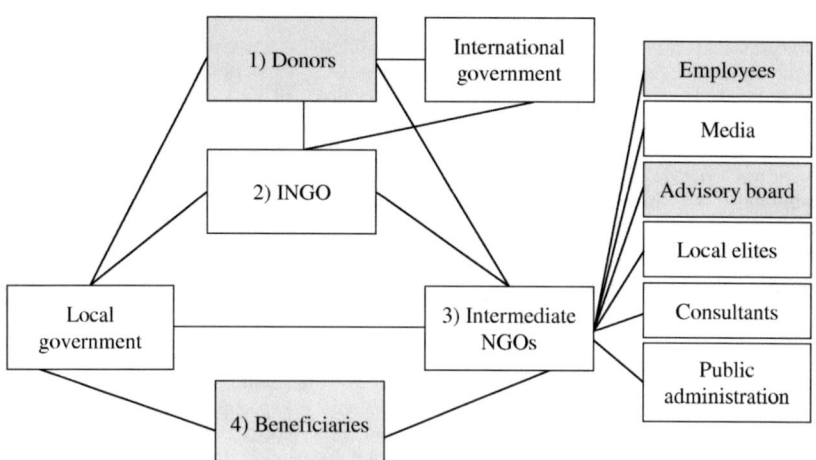

Source: modelled after Burger & Owens, 2013; Madon, 1999, p. 258; Smith, 2004, p. 2

4. Effectiveness of isomorphism in African non-governmental organizations

In this chapter the isomorphism caused by Western donors and its influence on effectiveness will be measured by using the model introduced in chapter 2.3. Therefore the chapter is divided into the four domains management, programs, environment and partnerships, to evaluate the influence on each of them.

In all four domains, coercive isomorphism, mainly caused by regulations and reporting requirements, is predominant. This is caused by the donors' geographical and political distance to African NGOs: Project visits are expensive and instead methods like quantifying, measuring and controlling NGOs by feedback forms, reports and audited financial statements are used to get information about the NGOs' work (Burger & Owens, 2013).

4.1 Management domain

The board and hence the employees working for the NGO are very much influenced by the donors (Hearn, 2007). Coercive isomorphism occurs for example because the donors shape the management's used structure, business plan and strategy. Michael wrote that African NGOs cannot set their own priorities, define their agendas or influence the international development community. Like a NGO leader in Clayés research (p.610) stated: "So if a donor says jump. You say how high and you do it." In the worst case Haveman (1993) stated, a from donor-side expected change in the leadership structure could lead to the NGO´s mortality. This can happen because often organizations and its enthusiastic, motivated, visionary leader are intimately intertwined (Sooryamoorthy & Gangrade, 2001). Moreover, the already mentioned bureaucratization can hinder decision making, limit the responsiveness of the NGO (Martens, 2002), create dependencies and undermine the NGOs empowerment (Hudock, 2001). Henderson (2002) claims that NGO managers often try hard to get grants to ensure their employees can stay. Even in on-site project implementation donors limit the management boards independence (Mundau & Tanga, 2014). To sum it up, donors expectations force NGOs to be more business-like by producing numbers which in contrast would prefer to act more on a trust basis (Claeyé & Jackson, 2012).

However, normative isomorphism brings positive aspects because donors support NGOs by sharing practices and innovation and reinforce the organizations learning (Ebrahim, 2003). They send expatriates (Sahara, 1991), offer programs to train the employees and sponsor trainings leading to more professionalization (Claeyé & Jackson, 2012). Moreover, other mechanisms for reducing poverty are technical assistance, capacity building, collaboration, publications, conferences, seminars and think thanks by i.e. the OECD (Foli & Béland, 2014). Of course it has to be considered that the trainings are often about the business-like approach and according to Esman (1988) do not necessarily lead to a better institutional capacity of the NGO but they also have many advantages such as idea exchange.

Also the third type of isomorphism, mimetic isomorphism, can be found in the management domain, when new NGOs mimic formal structures of established NGOs to gain acceptance from the group (Burger & Owens, 2013).

The three types of isomorphism in the management domain influence the three conceptualizations of effectiveness. Goals of the management board are on the one side negatively detached as the board cannot decide independently and has to focus on figures rather than on people. Nevertheless, if the board and donors agree on the same goals, the effects on effectiveness are positive. Thanks to donor funding it is easier to get resources and employees. The reputation depends on the satisfaction of the NGOs employees, the appearance of the management board in public and in relation to other stakeholders.

4.2 Program domain

Programs are the core element of NGOs to fulfill their mission of improving the beneficiaries' quality of life. In the following, isomorphism and its influences in projects are demonstrated. According to Mundau and Tanga (2014) there are positive and negative impacts of donor funding on recipients. The audit culture, an example for coercive isomorphism, can lead to focusing on inputs and contracts rather than on goals the NGOs try to reach (Burger & Owens, 2013). Hodson (1992) described it as moving away from pursuing a development mission to becoming a public service contractor working for donors. This means that short-term accountability towards donors about resources and immediate impact is more important than long-term accountability about the development impact for beneficiaries and the wider environment (Avina, 1993). Madon (1999) explains that it is difficult to satisfy both simultaneously. Moreover, through reporting expectations donors create a bureaucratization of development (Burger & Owens, 2013). If a NGO has to put much time in paper work and in learning the accountability requirements less time can be spent for projects (Mawdsley, Townsend, Porter, & Oakley, 2002). Many donors prefer easily quantifiable result oriented projects, which lead to a large number of short time-frame projects and hinders long-term sustainability (Ebrahim, 2003; Lindenberg & Bryant, 2001). Furthermore, donors influence the projects by determining their design and implementation (Smith, 2004). To put it in a nutshell, donors impact the project focus, the field work, as well as the terms and conditions, under which the projects are realized. Even the outcome and the evaluation of the project are influenced. This is likely to be against the NGOs mandate (Mundau & Tanga, 2014).

The mentioned examples demonstrate that donors can have negative effects on reaching the NGOs' goals. Due to the donors requirements NGOs cannot fulfill their own mission but have to adapt it to the donors expectations. This leads to a bad reputation in the community and towards donors. To sum up, coercive isomorphism can result into projects being less effective. Yet, although Western donors do not know the exact conditions on-site, they have better project experience, know how to work effectively and ensure project realization through funding. As a result, NGOs' projects can only be realized effectively through close cooperation in which NGOs share information from on-site and donors leave freedom for implementation.

4.3 Environment domain

The environment domain constitutes the organizational field in which the NGO operates. It mainly focuses on the NGOs' capability to secure resources in this field. A NGO which reaches its goals but is not good in report writing or which does not have connections to donors may lack funding opportunities (Burger & Owens, 2013; Mawdsley, Townsend, Porter, & Oakley, 2002). In the worst case, this may result in the closure of the NGO (Edwards & Hulme, 1995) as for many African NGOs the main determinant of survival is access to grants (Burger & Owens, 2013). And even if NGOs receive funding, this can lead to losing their strong presence in communities (Edwards & Hulme, 1995). The force of complying with Northern agendas led to a dependent NGO field in Africa (Wallace, 2003). But there are also advantages of coercive isomorphism. If NGOs already got grants and implemented structures donors expect, it will be more probable to be selected to support pilot projects (Claeyé & Jackson, 2012).

Institutional isomorphic pressure influences norms and standards in the field and what donors expect, so it has impact on what is seen as appropriate management in the NGO field. NGOs are lead to look at best practices and mimic managerialism, that are concepts like accountability, transparency, efficiency, strategic planning and project evaluation.

Managerialism emanates from global governance structures of donors. The fact that everything has to be documented is an apparent influence from Western donors. Resulting from mimetic isomorphism, the whole NGO environment becomes more business-like, with a trend to focus on outcome, using key performance indicators (KPIs) and behaving according to business etiquette and rules. To sum it up, the more formalized NGOs get, the more rules and regulations are to be followed. The only way to become more flexible and more responsive is an adjustment to the NGO field (Claeyé & Jackson, 2012). Consequently many NGOs moved to an implementation of donor funded projects and training of project members (Mundau & Tanga, 2014).

The analysis showed that cooperations with donors facilitate getting financial resources. At the same time, this may lead to a loose of the NGOs' strong presence in communities which in turn negatively influences their reputation.

4.4 Partnership domain

Partnerships are i.e. possible between NGOs and donors, governments, other NGOs, and companies. Especially North-South partnerships between African NGOs and donors are considered as enablers for more efficient use of scarce resources resulting in increased sustainability (Lister, 2000). However, often the Western projects do not fit with the culture abroad (Lindenberg & Bryant, 2001) and power inequality between both arises (Lister, 2000). According to the principal agent theory donors act as principals telling NGOs (agents) what to do. They try to "match the West with Africa" (Claeyé & Jackson, 2012, p. 607). Moreover, partners have their own focus areas i.e. environment or focus regions in which they exclusively invest (Rauh, 2010) so that local suggestions of focus areas are often ignored. To conclude, in partnerships coercive isomorphism is dominating.

Also in networks coercive isomorphism can occur when donors expect NGOs to join i.e. the ECNGOC (Eastern Cape NGO Coalition) to adhere to the code of ethics showing that they use proper organizational structures and practices. This means to subscribe to five out of the six principles, values, governance, accountability, management and human resources, finances and resources (Claeyé & Jackson, 2012; ECNGOC, 2015). In networks moreover mimetic isomorphism occurs when NGOs get information from their partner or copy them (Claeyé & Jackson, 2012) and normative isomorphism comes up when they learn from each other, which results in a professionalization.

If the goals of the partners, in this case the donors and NGOs, are in line this can have a positive impact on the goals' effectiveness. Moreover, resources are secured by donor relationships. The participation in networks like the ECNGOC might positively influence the NGOs' reputation. Abrahamsen (2004) sums up that the power of partnerships is voluntary and coercive at the same time.

5. Conclusion

To conclude the outcome of isomorphism is that African NGOs became "local managers of foreign aid money, not managers of local African development processes" (Nyang'oro, 1993, p. 288). As demonstrated in chapter four, there are all types of isomorphism in the African NGO field whereby coercive isomorphism is dominant. Summarizing the findings, isomorphism through Western donors does not lead automatically to more effectiveness. There are many negative outcomes of audit culture and the influence of donors is too big. Although the reporting and accountability processes have been criticized broadly, NGOs widely adopted them. Institutional theory explains this with legitimating industry norms and power imbalance between donors and NGOs. However, many projects could not be realized without funding. Therefore, a fundamental requirement for NGOs is grants.

Nevertheless, to a certain extent NGOs should negotiate and resist to what donors expect because bureaucracy, business-orientation and short-term focus will not result in NGO effectiveness. Consequently, a middle course has to be found as generally donors follow the same aim as NGOs, to help those in need. The NGOs should keep their visionary view on their mission and only let influence their work by isomorphism to a certain extent. Meetings between the NGOs and donors should be arranged to discuss the problem of isomorphism caused by Western donors. Ideas, links to beneficiaries and local knowledge from NGOs should be used to realize more effective projects.

In the end some limitations have to be considered. First, the paper did not offer an in-depth, country-specific analysis of donor influence and assumes that donor influence on NGOs is the same in all African countries. This is in real life not possible as the parts of Africa have very different economic and living conditions as well as a varying amount of funding. Second, there is a need for detailed and large panel data for a reliable research. Another important research area would be the aspects donors should look at for choosing effectiveness promising NGOs.

References

Abrahamsen, R. (2004). The Power of Partnerships in Global Governance. *Third World Quarterly, 25*(8), 1453–1467. doi:10.2307/3993796

Avina, J. (1993). The evolutionary life cycles of non-governmental development organizations. *Public Administration and Development, 13*(5), 453–474. doi:10.1002/pad.4230130502

Burger, R., & Owens, T. (2013). Receive Grants or Perish?: The Survival Prospects of Ugandan Non-Governmental Organisations. *Journal of Development Studies, 49*(9), 1284–1298. doi:10.1080/00220388.2012.754430

Carroll, G. R., & Delacroix, J. (1982). Organizational Mortality in the Newspaper Industries of Argentina and Ireland: An Ecological Approach. *Administrative Science Quarterly, 27*(2), 169–198. doi:10.2307/2392299

Claeyé, F., & Jackson, T. (2012). The Iron Cage Re-Revisited: Institutional Isomorphism in Non-profit Organisations in South-Africa. *Journal of International Development, 24*(5), 602–622. doi:10.1002/jid.2852

DiMaggio, P. J., & Powell, W. W. (1983). The Iron Cage Revisited: Institutional Isomorphism and Collective Rationality in Organizational Fields. *American Sociological Review, 48*(2), 147–160. doi:10.2307/2095101

Ebrahim, A. (2003). Accountability In Practice: Mechanisms for NGOs. *World Development, 31*(5), 813–829. doi:10.1016/S0305-750X(03)00014-7

ECNGOC. (2015). *Eastern Cape Non-Governmental Coalition: Principles of the ECNGOC Code of Ethics.* Retrieved from http://ecngoc.co.za/index.php?option=com_content&view=category&layout=blog&id=70&Itemid=159

Edwards, M., & Hulme, D. (1995). *Non-governmental Organisations: Performance and Accountability Beyond the Magic Bullet. An Earthscan original*: Earthscan. Retrieved from https://books.google.de/books?id=68r6eaVQ78AC

Esman, M. J. (1988). The maturing of development administration. *Public Administration and Development, 8*(2), 125–134. doi:10.1002/pad.4230080202

Fennell, M. L. (1980). The Effects of Environmental Characteristics on the Structure of Hospital Clusters. *Administrative Science Quarterly, 25*(3), 485. doi:10.2307/2392265

Foli, R., & Béland, D. (2014). International Organizations and Ideas About Poverty in Sub-Saharan Africa. *Poverty & Public Policy, 6*(1), 3–23. doi:10.1002/pop4.62

Hager, M., Galaskiewicz, J., Bielefeld, W., & Pins, J. (1996). Tales From the Grave: Organizations' Accounts of Their Own Demise HAGER,. *American Behavioral Scientist, 39*(8), 975–994. doi:10.1177/0002764296039008004

Haveman, H. A. (1993). Ghosts of Managers Past: Managerial Succession and Organizational Mortality. *The Academy of Management Journal, 36*(4), 864–881. doi:10.2307/256762

Hearn, J. (2007). African NGOs: The New Compradors? *Development and Change, 38*(6), 1095–1110. doi:10.1111/j.1467-7660.2007.00447.x

Henderson, S. (2002). Selling Civil Society: Western Aid and the Nongovernmental Organization Sector in Russia. *Comparative Political Studies, 35*(2), 139–167. doi:10.1177/0010414002035002001

Hodson, R. (1992). Small, medium or lrage? The rocky road to NGO growth. In M. Edwards & D. Hulme (Eds.), *Making a difference. NGOs and development in a changing world* . London, Washington, DC: Earthscan Publications.

Hudock, A. (2001). *NGOs and civil society: Democracy by proxy?* Malden, MA: Polity Press.

Kontinen, T. (Ed.) 2005. *Institutional isomorphism and small non-governmental organisations in Tanzania.*

Lecy, J. D., Schmitz, H. P., & Swedlund, H. (2012). Non-Governmental and Not-for-Profit Organizational Effectiveness: A Modern Synthesis. *VOLUNTAS: International Journal of Voluntary and Nonprofit Organizations, 23*(2), 434–457. doi:10.1007/s11266-011-9204-6

Lindenberg, M., & Bryant, C. (2001). *Going global: Transforming relief and development NGOs.* Bloomfield, CT: Kumarian Press.

Lister, S. (2000). Power in partnership? An analysis of an NGO's relationships with its partners. *Journal of International Development, (12)*, 227–239.

Madon, S. (1999). International NGOs: Networking, information flows and learning. *The Journal of Strategic Information Systems, 8*(3), 251–261. doi:10.1016/S0963-8687(99)00029-3

Martens, B. (2002). *The institutional economics of foreign aid.* New York: Cambridge University Press.

Mawdsley, E., Townsend, J., Porter, G., & Oakley, P. (2002). *Knowledge, power and development agendas: NGOs North and South. INTRAC NGO management & policy series: no. 14.* Oxford: INTRAC.

Meyer, J. W., & Hannan, M. T. (1979). *National development and the world system: Educational, economic, and political change, 1950-1970.* Chicago: University of Chicago Press.

Michael, S. (2004). *Undermining Development: The Absence of Power Among Local Ngos in Africa.* Oxford: James Currey and Bloomington: Indiana University Press.

Mundau, M., & Tanga, P. T. (2014). The Impact of Donor-funded Community Empowerment Projects on Poverty Alleviation in Zimbabwe. *Perspectives on Global Development and Technology, 13*(4), 465–480. doi:10.1163/15691497-12341312

Muturi, D., & Parris, A. (2013). Improving processes for good in East Africa. *The TQM Journal, 25*(5), 458–472. doi:10.1108/TQM-11-2012-0101

Nelson, P. (2006). The varied and conditional integration of NGOs in the aid system: NGOs and the World Bank. *Journal of International Development, 18*(5), 701–713. doi:10.1002/jid.1302

North, D. C. (1990). *Institutions, institutional change, and economic performance. The Political economy of institutions and decisions.* Cambridge, New York: Cambridge University Press.

Nyang'oro, J. E. (1993). Development, Democracy and NGOs in Africa. *Scandinavian Journal of Development Alternatives, 12*(2-3), 277–291.

Rauh, K. (2010). NGOs, Foreign Donors, and Organizational Processes: Passive NGO Recipients or Strategic Actors? *McGill Sociological Review, 1*, 29–45. Retrieved from https://www.mcgill.ca/msr/volume1/article2

Sahara, T. (1991). Donor Delivery Style, Learning, and Institutional Development. *Journal of Management Development, 10*(6), 60–83. doi:10.1108/02621719110139908

Sellers, R. D., Fogarty, T. J., & Parker, L. M. (2012). Unleashing the Technical Core: Institutional Theory and the Aftermath of Arthur Andersen. *Behavioral Research in Accounting, 24*(1), 181–201. doi:10.2308/bria-10176

Smith, S. C. (2004). Governance of Nongovernmental Organizations: A Framework and Application to Poverty Programs in East Africa. *SSRN Electronic Journal.* doi:10.2139/ssrn.628684

Sooryamoorthy, R., & Gangrade, K. D. (2001). *NGOs in India: A cross-sectional study. Contributions in sociology: no. 136.* Westport, Conn.: Greenwood Press.

Sudit, E. F. (1996). *Effectiveness, quality, and efficiency: A management oriented approach.* Boston, Norwell, Mass.: Kluwer Academic Publishers; Distributors for North America, Kluwer Academic Publishers.

United Nations. (2013). *Nichtregierungsorganisationen (NGOs) und die Vereinten Nationen.* Retrieved from http://www.unric.org/de/aufbau-der-uno/85

Vakil, A. C. (1997). Confronting the classification problem: Toward a taxonomy of NGOs. *World Development, 25*(12), 2057–2070. doi:10.1016/S0305-750X(97)00098-3

Wallace, T. (2003). NGO Dilemmas: Trojan Horses for Global Neoliberalism? In L. Panitch & C. Leys (Eds.), *Socialist Register 2004: The New Imperial Challenge* . London: Merlin.

World Bank. (1995). *Working with NGOs A Practical Guide to Operational Collaboration between the World Bank and Non-Governmental Organizations.*